WALKING THROUGH GRIEF, UNDERSTANDING AND HEALING THROUGH THE FIVE STAGES

A Cornerstone Funeral Services & Cremations Guide

Grief Forward™ Manual: Walking Through Grief, Understanding and Healing Through the Five Stages

A Cornerstone Funeral Services & Cremations Resource
Part of the Grief Forward™ Series

Copyright © 2025 Cornerstone Funeral Services & Cremations
All rights reserved.

No part of this publication may be reproduced, distributed, or transmitted in any form or by any means, including photocopying, recording, scanning, or other electronic or mechanical methods, without the prior written permission of the publisher, except in the case of brief quotations used in critical reviews, educational contexts, or other noncommercial uses permitted by copyright law.

All scriptures, references, and quotations are used respectfully for educational and inspirational purposes

For permission requests, contact:
Cornerstone Funeral Services & Cremations
2416 Carson Road
Birmingham, AL 35215
Phone: (205) 949-9500
Mobile: (205)-917-9658
www.cfs-c.com

ISBN: 979-8-90155-518-7
Printed in Birmingham, AL

Disclaimer: This book is intended for educational and informational purposes only. It is not a substitute for professional medical, therapeutic, or counseling advice. Readers are encouraged to consult qualified professionals for support. The author and publisher disclaim liability for any adverse outcomes arising from the use of this material.

Trademark Notice: Grief Forward™ are trademarks of Cornerstone Funeral Services & Cremations. All rights reserved. Unauthorized use of the name, logo, or program materials is prohibited by law.

grief Forward™ manual

WALKING THROUGH GRIEF, UNDERSTANDING AND HEALING THROUGH THE FIVE STAGES

A Cornerstone Funeral Services & Cremations Guide

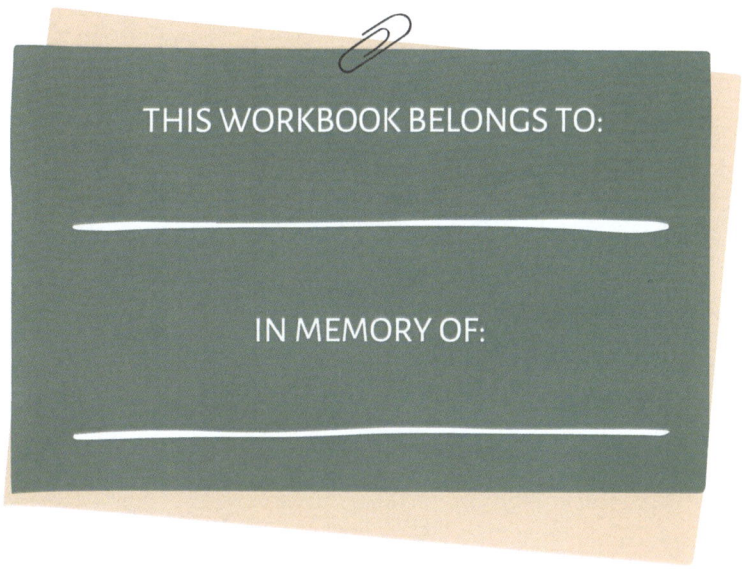

THIS WORKBOOK BELONGS TO:

_____

IN MEMORY OF:

_____

Healing isn't rushed... it's supported."

DEDICATION

This book is dedicated to every heart learning to live with loss.

To those who are grieving quietly, to those who are grieving loudly, to those who carry their pain in silence, and to those who are doing the best they can one day, one moment, one breath at a time.

To the families I have served, who have taught me the true meaning of courage, love, and resilience. Your stories, your tears, and your strength have shaped this work in ways words cannot express.

To anyone who has ever felt alone in their grief —may this book remind you that healing is possible, that your feelings are valid, and that you do not have to walk this journey by yourself.

And to my own family, whose love grounds me, strengthens me, and inspires everything I do.

This is for you.

Table Of Contents

INTRODUCTION	1
CHAPTER 1: STAGE ONE - DENIAL	3
CHAPTER 2: STAGE TWO - ANGER	15
CHAPTER 3: STAGE THREE - BARGAINING	27
CHAPTER 4: STAGE FOUR - DEPRESSION	39
CHAPTER 5: STAGE FIVE - ACCEPTANCE	57
HEALING TOOLS, ACTIVITIES & DAILY PRACTICES	75
CHAPTER 6 - A NEW PATH FORWARD	81
RESOURCE GUIDE	85
REFERENCES	92
ACKNOWLEDGMENTS	93
ABOUT THE AUTHOR	94

WHY I WROTE THIS BOOK

Grief is a journey I have witnessed up close — not only through the families I've had the honor of serving, but through the countless stories, tears, questions, and moments of quiet strength shared across my career in funeral service. Every day, I meet people whose lives have been changed in an instant. People who walk through the doors of Cornerstone Funeral Services overwhelmed, hurting, afraid, and unsure of what tomorrow will bring.

Time and time again, I have seen one truth rise above everything else:
People need support long after the funeral is over.

Families often tell me they feel alone. Teens say they don't know how to express what they are feeling. Adults wonder if they're grieving "the right way." Some try to stay busy, others shut down, and many assume their grief should be hidden or healed by a certain timeline. But grief doesn't follow rules. It doesn't move in a straight line. And it certainly doesn't disappear just because life keeps going.

This book was created to help fill that gap — to give individuals and families a compassionate guide long after the service ends and the crowd goes home. Grief Forward™ is designed to bring comfort, understanding, and direction to those who feel lost in the heaviness of loss. It is here to remind you that grief doesn't need to be rushed... but it does need to be supported.

My hope is that these pages meet you exactly where you are: whether newly grieving, processing long-held pain, or learning how to carry your loss with grace. I wrote this book to honor every person who has ever walked into my care, every story that touched my heart, and every soul who needed help navigating life after loss.

To grieve is to love. To heal is to honor that love in a new way. And to move forward — not away — is the ultimate act of courage.

If you are holding this book, I want you to know: You are not alone. Your feelings are valid. And healing is possible, one gentle step at a time.

This is not just a guide. This is a companion.

This is your invitation to move forward —
Grief Forward™.

Bernard C. Buggs, Jr., CFSP, CCO, CPC
Owner & Licensed Funeral Director

BERNARD C. BUGGS, JR.
CFSP, CCO, CPC
OWNER

"The Lord is close to the brokenhearted and saves those who are crushed in spirit."

— Psalm 34:18

CHAPTER 1: STAGE ONE

Denial

For I am convinced that neither death nor life, neither angels nor demons, neither the present nor the future, nor any powers, neither height nor depth, nor anything else in all creation, will be able to separate us from the love of God that is in Christ Jesus our Lord.

— Romans 8:38-39

Understanding Denial

Denial is the mind's gentle way of saying, "Not yet." When loss first happens—whether through death, a breakup, trauma, or life-changing news—our hearts simply cannot absorb the full weight of reality all at once. The world feels unfamiliar, and nothing seems to make sense.

In this early stage, many people move through their days on autopilot. Meals are eaten without tasting them. Conversations feel distant. Time seems to slow down and blur together. Denial is not a character flaw, nor is it an attempt to ignore truth. Instead, it is the brain's natural defense mechanism—a protective emotional cushion that allows us to take in life's hardest truths gradually.

> Psychiatrist Elisabeth Kübler-Ross, who developed the Five Stages of Grief model, described denial as the body and mind's first response to loss: a temporary space of emotional safety that gives us time to breathe.

How Denial Shows Up

Denial does not look the same for everyone. Some people experience it subtly, while others feel it intensely during the first days or weeks after a loss.

Denial may appear in the following ways:

- Emotional numbness — feeling disconnected or unable to cry.
- Continuing routines as if nothing happened — work, chores, or school may offer a false sense of normalcy.
- Avoiding conversations about the loss or changing the subject when feelings arise.
- Minimizing or intellectualizing — saying things like, "I'm fine," "It will make sense later," or "It wasn't that bad," even when the pain is very real.
- Keeping life unchanged — such as leaving a loved one's room untouched or expecting them to walk through the door.

A Relatable Example: A woman who has lost her spouse may still set two plates at the dinner table without thinking. She is not confused; she is grieving. Her heart has not yet caught up with her reality, and her routines temporarily help her survive the early days of loss.

Why Denial Is Necessary

Denial protects us from becoming emotionally overwhelmed. The human brain is designed to guard us from shock, especially during moments of trauma or life-altering change.

Why denial matters:

- It softens the blow of painful news.
- It creates a buffer that prevents emotional overload.
- It allows us to function in daily life while processing grief little by little.
- It gives the mind time to adjust gradually, preventing collapse or panic.

Modern psychology and trauma research show that denial is not the refusal to feel; it is the body's way of letting reality in slowly, one heartbeat at a time.

Reflection Thought:

"Denial is the mind's way of offering shelter until the storm passes enough for us to see the sky again."

Signs You Are Moving Through Denial

Denial does not end suddenly—it shifts gradually. Many people do not realize they have moved through this stage until they look back and see the changes.

Signs that healing is beginning:

- You start speaking about the loss using real terms: "She passed," "The relationship is over," "This happened to me."
- You feel waves of emotion—sadness, anger, confusion—which means your heart is awakening to the truth.
- You begin looking for meaning, information, or understanding.
- You notice small changes in your routines, such as putting away certain items or acknowledging anniversaries.
- You begin reaching out for support or allowing others to comfort you.

> These moments are not setbacks - they are signs of courage. Feeling more emotion often means denial is loosening its hold, and your heart is preparing for deeper healing.

Healthy vs. Unhealthy Denial

Denial, when temporary, is healthy and protective. But when it lingers too long, it can become a barrier to healing.

Healthy Denial

- Helps you survive the shock.
- Lasts temporarily—days, weeks, or sometimes a few months.
- Shifts as you begin to process emotions.
- Allows slow, steady acceptance of reality.

Unhealthy or Chronic Denial

- Refusing to acknowledge the loss for long periods.
- Avoiding all conversations related to what happened.
- Using substances or distractions to silence emotions.
- Refusing support from family, faith leaders, or professionals.
- Becoming emotionally stuck—unable to move forward.

If denial becomes a long-term pattern, it may indicate deeper emotional wounds that require support from a grief counselor, therapist, or trusted professional.

Coping Strategies: Moving Forward With Grace

You cannot force yourself out of denial. Healing begins when you gently invite honesty, awareness, and compassion into your life.

Practical Ways to Cope:

- Journal what feels real today. Write without judgment.
- Talk with someone you trust—a friend, pastor, or counselor.
- Create small rituals that acknowledge the loss (lighting a candle, praying, visiting a meaningful place).
- Practice grounding exercises:
    - Deep breathing
    - Naming five things you see
    - Placing your hand on your heart and saying, "I am safe."

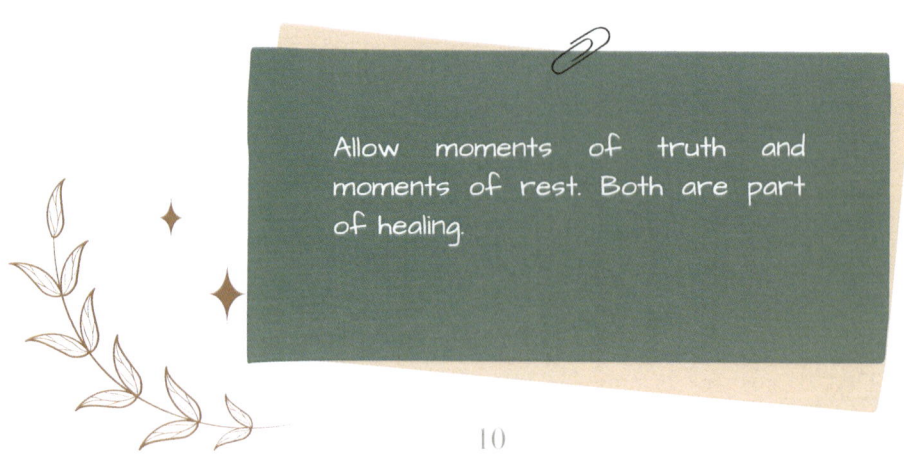

Allow moments of truth and moments of rest. Both are part of healing.

Reflection, Healing, and Hope

Denial is often the first doorway into grief. It creates space for you to breathe while your world rearranges itself. As you slowly step through this stage, emotions like anger, sadness, fear, or confusion may begin to surface. This is not weakness—it is progress.

Moving beyond denial does not mean forgetting the person, relationship, or life you lost. It is an act of self-compassion, a sign that your heart is beginning to heal and that you are learning to carry your love forward in a new form.

> Denial softens the initial blow of grief. When the fog begins to lift, deeper emotions emerge. The next stage - Anger, often rises as reality becomes clearer. While challenging, it is a natural and meaningful part of healing.

Healing Exercise

Write a letter to yourself describing the loss—but only express what your heart is ready to accept today. You do not have to force full acceptance. Simply honor your current truth with kindness.

Notes & Personal Reflections

What moments of denial do I recognize in myself?

What truths am I slowly becoming ready to accept?

What support do I need during this stage?

What memories or moments feel the hardest to face right now?

"The Lord upholds all who fall and lifts up all who are bowed down."

— Psalm 145:14

CHAPTER 2: STAGE TWO

Anger

"Blessed are those who mourn, for they will be comforted."

— Matthew 5:4

Understanding Anger in Grief

Anger is often misunderstood, yet it is one of the most natural responses to loss. When denial begins to fade and reality becomes clearer, the heart shifts into a stage where the pain needs a voice. That voice often emerges as anger.

Anger does not mean you are "losing control" or "not coping well." In grief, anger is a sign that your heart has awakened to the depth of what has changed. The feelings may come suddenly, without warning. You may feel anger at the situation, at the illness or event that caused the loss, at yourself, at God, or even at the person who died or left.

It is important to remember: anger in grief is not a moral failure—it is an emotional release that helps the heart slowly make sense of suffering.

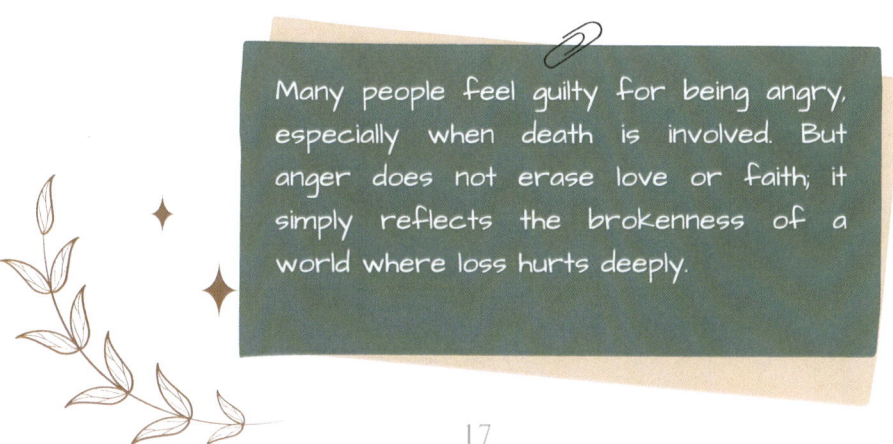

Many people feel guilty for being angry, especially when death is involved. But anger does not erase love or faith; it simply reflects the brokenness of a world where loss hurts deeply.

How Anger Manifests

Anger can surface in many forms. Some expressions are loud and visible; others are quiet and internal.

Grieving individuals may feel:

- Irritability or frustration over small things.
- Anger at doctors, circumstances, or systems that "should have done more."
- Resentment toward people who seem unaffected or who move on quickly.
- Blame placed on oneself or others.
- Anger at God or faith struggles: "Why would God let this happen?"
- Internal anger, such as shame, guilt, or self-criticism.

Common Behaviors:

- Snapping at others
- Withdrawal or shutting down
- Feeling overwhelmed by life's demands
- Replaying events over and over, searching for someone to blame

A Relatable Example: A father grieving the loss of his daughter might find himself frustrated at coworkers who laugh or talk normally. The world moves on—but he cannot. His anger is not truly about them; it is about the hole that grief has carved inside him.

The Purpose of Anger

While anger feels uncomfortable, it serves several healing purposes:

Anger Creates Movement
It breaks through the emotional numbness of denial. You begin to feel again—even if those feelings are heavy. This is progress.

Anger Gives Grief a Voice
Anger expresses the injustice, the pain, and the questions the heart is wrestling with. It turns silent suffering into expressed emotion.

Anger Helps Us Seek Meaning
You may begin asking: "Why did this happen?" "Could things have been different?" These questions are a part of making sense of the loss.

Anger Protects Emotional Wounds
Sometimes anger shields you from deeper emotions like fear or sorrow until you're ready to feel them.

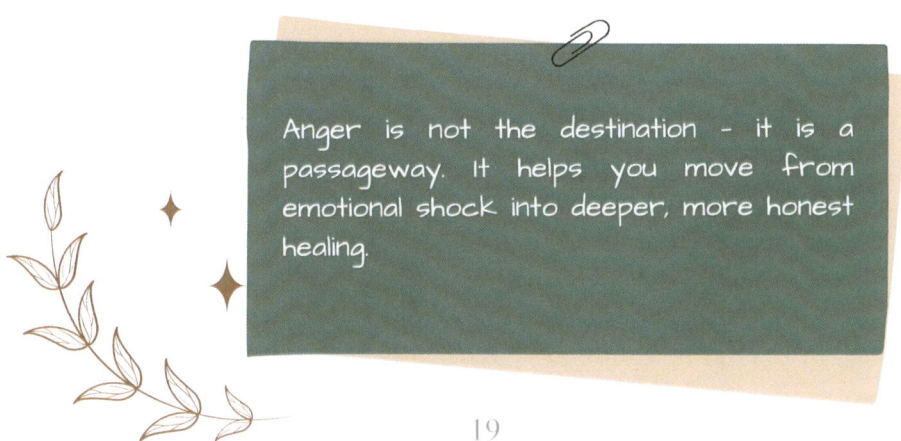

Anger is not the destination - it is a passageway. It helps you move from emotional shock into deeper, more honest healing.

Healthy vs. Unhealthy Expressions of Anger

Anger becomes harmful only when it is directed in destructive ways or when it masks your true pain for too long.

Healthy Anger

- Expressing emotions through talking, journaling, or crying
- Acknowledging the hurt without self-blame or harming others
- Feeling anger come and go in waves
- Using anger as a tool to understand your grief
- Seeking support when emotions feel heavy

Unhealthy Anger

- Lashing out at loved ones
- Using substances to numb feelings
- Self-harm or extreme risk-taking
- Refusing to talk about the loss
- Constantly blaming yourself or others
- Becoming stuck in resentment

> Healthy anger helps you release.
>
> Unhealthy anger keeps you trapped. Recognizing the difference is a step toward deeper healing.

What Anger Is Really Trying to Tell You

Anger is usually a surface emotion—a protector guarding something more vulnerable underneath.

In grief, anger may be covering:

- Fear of facing life without the person or situation you lost
- Sorrow that feels too heavy to carry
- Disbelief that something so painful has happened
- Guilt or "what if" thoughts
- Powerlessness when life feels unpredictable

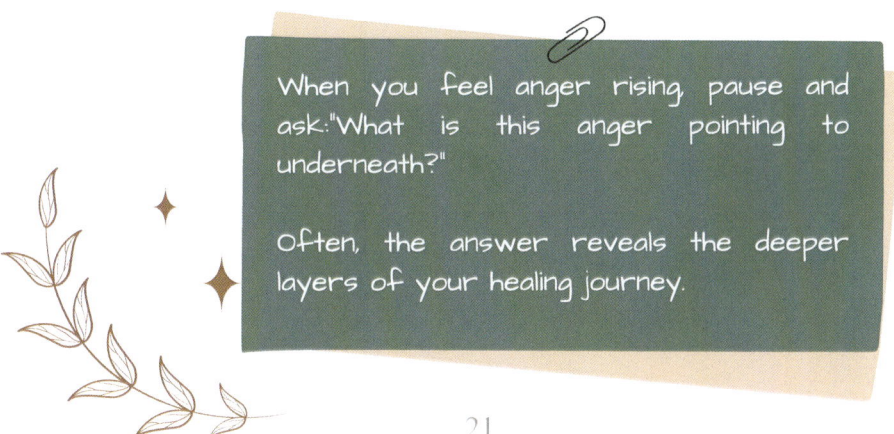

When you feel anger rising, pause and ask: "What is this anger pointing to underneath?"

Often, the answer reveals the deeper layers of your healing journey.

Ways to Cope and Move Forward

These coping tools help channel anger in healthy and meaningful ways:

Name Your Anger
Say to yourself: "I am angry because..." Labeling emotions reduces their intensity.

Practice Safe Release
- Write furiously in a journal
- Go for a brisk walk
- Cry loudly in a private space
- Squeeze a pillow
- Do deep breathing exercises

Talk to Someone You Trust
Share your frustration with someone who will listen without judgment.

Redirect Energy Into Something Meaningful
Creative outlets—drawing, music, cooking, exercise—help transform anger into expression.

Use Mindfulness and Grounding
Pause and breathe. Feel your feet on the ground. Remind yourself: "I am safe. I am hurting, but I am healing."

Seek Spiritual or Professional Support
Pastors, counselors, and grief specialists can guide you through heavier emotions.

Healing Exercise

Write a list of everything you're angry about. Then circle the items that actually reflect grief, fear, or love beneath the anger. This helps reveal the heart's true needs.

Reflection, Healing, and Hope

Anger may feel uncomfortable, but it is a powerful sign that your healing has begun. It means your heart is waking up to the truth of what you've lost, and it is searching for meaning and justice in a world that suddenly feels unfair.

As you learn to express anger in healthy ways, the intensity will soften. You will begin to uncover the deeper emotions beneath it—sadness, longing, fear, love. These are not signs of weakness; they are signs of being human.

Anger will not last forever. It is a bridge that carries you toward honesty, toward connection, and toward acceptance. When this stage begins to quiet, many people find themselves entering the next stage of grief—Bargaining—where the mind tries to make sense of what has happened through "if only" thoughts and searching for answers.

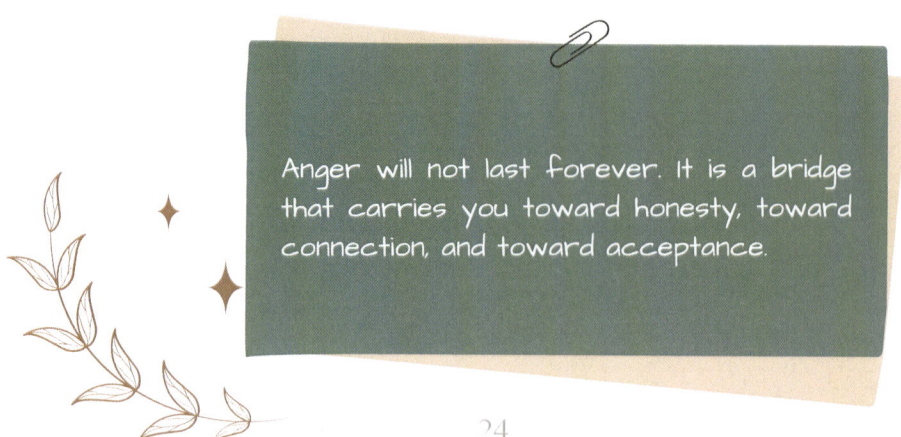

Anger will not last forever. It is a bridge that carries you toward honesty, toward connection, and toward acceptance.

Notes & Personal Reflections

What am I angry about today?

What might this anger be protecting underneath?

Who or what feels "responsible" for the pain I'm in?

What healthy outlets help me release anger?

What have I learned about myself in this stage?

"So do not fear, for I am with you; do not be dismayed, for I am your God. I will strengthen you and help you; I will uphold you with my righteous right hand."

— Isaiah 41:10

CHAPTER 3: STAGE THREE

Bargaining

"He heals the brokenhearted and binds up their wounds."

— Psalm 147:3

Understanding Bargaining

Bargaining is the stage where the mind searches for answers, solutions, and "what could have been." After the intensity of anger begins to ease, the heart often tries to regain a sense of control. This happens through mental negotiations such as:

- "If only I had done something differently..."
- "Maybe if I change this or that, things will feel normal again."
- "I should have said more... stayed longer... noticed sooner."

Bargaining is not about blame—it is about longing. It's the heart trying to rewrite reality because the real version hurts too much. This stage often brings emotional complexity: regret, guilt, self-questioning, and deep yearning for what was lost.

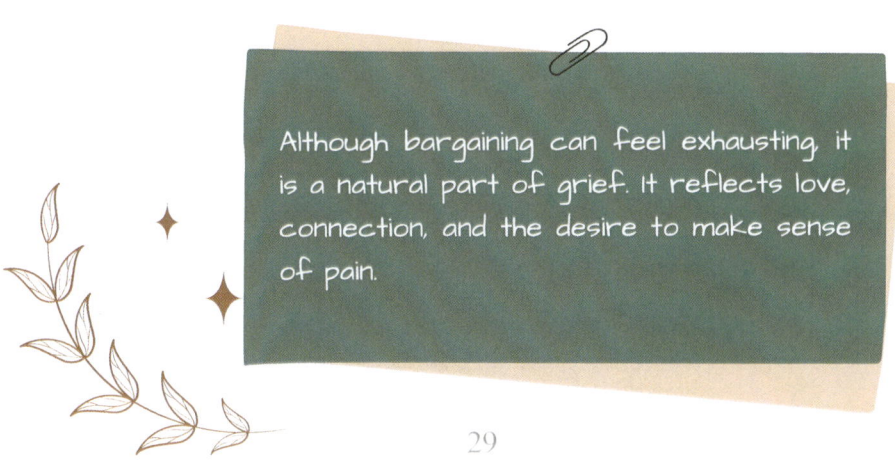

Although bargaining can feel exhausting, it is a natural part of grief. It reflects love, connection, and the desire to make sense of pain.

How Bargaining Manifests

Bargaining may show up in emotional, mental, or behavioral ways.

People in this stage often:

- Replay events repeatedly, searching for a different outcome
- Ask themselves "why" and "what if" questions
- Make promises to God or themselves
- Imagine scenarios where the loss could have been prevented
- Feel regret for past conversations or actions
- Experience intrusive or looping thoughts
- Seek reassurance from others

> A daughter who loses her father may replay their last conversation over and over, wishing she had stayed longer or said more. She knows she cannot change the past, but her heart is trying to stay connected to him by revisiting the moments they shared.

Why Bargaining Happens

Bargaining is rooted in the search for control. Loss makes life feel unpredictable and chaotic, which humans naturally resist. The mind tries to make sense of the pain through reflection, questioning, and sometimes self-blame.

Purpose of Bargaining

- It allows the heart to process regret and longing.
- It helps us gradually face reality by mentally approaching it from different angles.
- It reveals how deeply we loved, cared, or hoped.
- It gives the mind space to confront the "unrealness" of loss.
- It initiates the internal work of finding meaning and understanding.

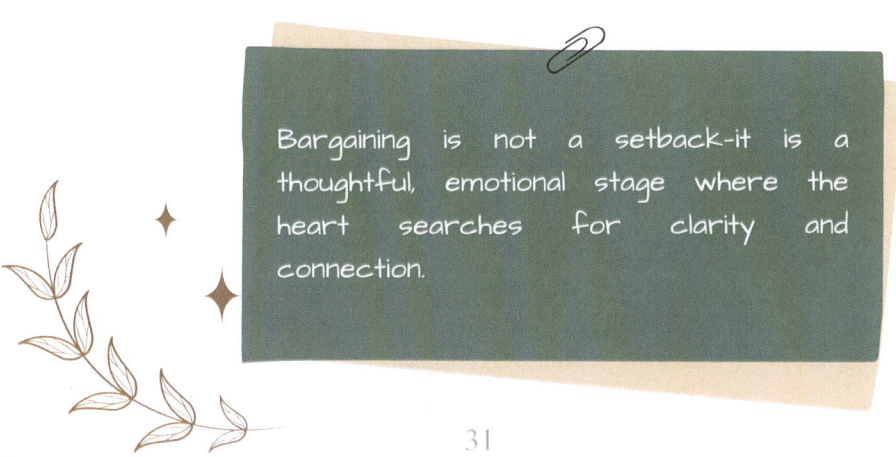

Bargaining is not a setback-it is a thoughtful, emotional stage where the heart searches for clarity and connection.

The Emotional Complexity of Bargaining

Bargaining often opens the door to several layered emotions:

1. Regret
Wishing we had known more or done more.

2. Guilt
Taking responsibility for things that were not actually in our control.

3. Longing
Wishing for one more day, one more hug, one more chance.

4. Confusion
Struggling to understand the "why" behind the loss.

5. Hope for impossible outcomes
A desire to rewind time, prevent the loss, or change the story.

Most of the thoughts in this stage are fueled by love, not logic. They reveal the depth of the relationship or situation that has changed.

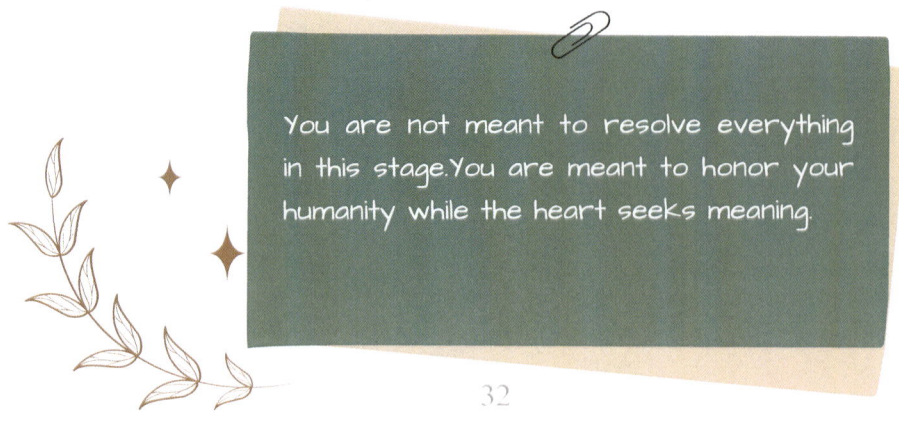

You are not meant to resolve everything in this stage. You are meant to honor your humanity while the heart seeks meaning.

When Bargaining Becomes Unhealthy

Most people move through bargaining naturally, but it can become harmful if it turns into persistent self-blame or rumination.

Unhealthy Bargaining Looks Like:

- Constantly blaming yourself for what happened
- Rewriting the past in ways that shame you
- Becoming stuck in regret for months or years
- Believing you caused the loss
- Making promises rooted in fear instead of healing
- Obsessively revisiting events without relief

If the mind becomes trapped in self-punishment, counseling or grief support can help break the cycle and offer healthier pathways toward acceptance.

Healthy Bargaining Involves:

- Recognizing which thoughts are realistic vs. emotional
- Allowing yourself grace as you revisit memories
- Accepting that you did what you could with what you knew at the time
- Understanding that grief is not a problem to solve—it is an experience to move through

Coping Strategies: How to Move Forward

Bargaining improves when we gently create space for truth, compassion, and acceptance. Here are helpful ways to move through this stage:

1. Write Down Your "What If" Thoughts
Seeing them on paper helps separate emotion from reality.

2. Challenge Unrealistic Blame
Ask yourself: "Is this truly my fault, or is this grief talking?"

3. Talk Through Regret With Someone Safe
A trusted friend, pastor, or therapist can help you view the situation with kindness and clarity.

4. Practice Self-Compassion
Offer yourself the same forgiveness you would give someone you love.

5. Honor the Love Behind the Regret
Often, bargaining thoughts reflect how much the relationship or dream meant to you.

6. Spiritual or Mindfulness Practices
Prayer, meditation, grounding exercises, or quiet reflection can reduce overwhelm.

Healing Exercise

Write a compassionate letter to your past self, acknowledging what you did right, not just what you wish you did differently.

Reflection, Healing, and Hope

Bargaining is often the quiet, internal stage of grief. The questions you ask yourself come from a place of love, longing, and the desire to rewrite what cannot be changed. As painful as this stage can be, it softens over time.

When you begin accepting that the past cannot be undone—and when self-blame loosens its grip—you will notice moments where truth feels a little lighter. These moments signal movement toward the next stage of grief: Depression, where the weight of the loss settles in and deeper emotional processing takes place.

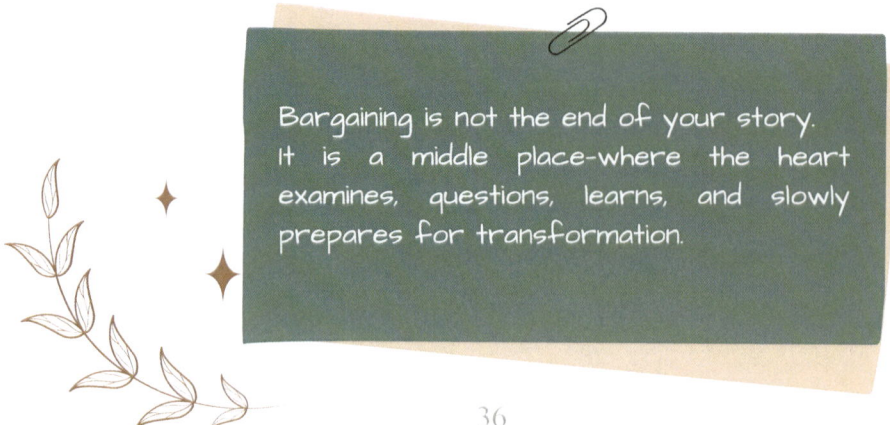

Bargaining is not the end of your story. It is a middle place-where the heart examines, questions, learns, and slowly prepares for transformation.

Notes & Personal Reflections

What "what if" or "if only" thoughts do I repeat most?

Which of these thoughts come from regret versus grief?

What would I say to my past self with compassion?

What truth am I slowly beginning to accept?

What meaning or understanding am I searching for?

"The righteous cry out, and the Lord hears them; he delivers them from all their troubles."

— Psalm 34:17

CHAPTER 4: STAGE FOUR

Depression

"He gives strength to the weary and increases the power of the weak."

— Isaiah 40:29

A Deeper Look at Depression in Grief

Depression in grief is often misunderstood, feared, or mislabeled. Many people assume it means something is "wrong" with them or that they are not coping correctly. But in the grieving process, depression is a deeply human response — a sign that your heart has finally reached the point where it can sit with the truth of your loss.

This stage does not arrive suddenly. It quietly emerges as denial fades, anger softens, and bargaining exhausts the mind. When the full weight of the loss sinks in, sadness naturally rises.

This form of depression is not emotional weakness. It is emotional honesty.

> You feel the emptiness because the loss mattered. You feel the heaviness because the relationship or situation shaped your life. You feel the sorrow because love leaves an imprint that the heart must learn to carry.

The Emotional Terrain of Grief-Related Depression

This stage brings a range of feelings, many of which may shift from day to day or hour to hour:

Common Emotional Experiences

- Persistent sadness or tearfulness
- Emotional numbness or flatness
- Loneliness, even around others
- A deep ache or emptiness
- Difficulty experiencing joy
- Feelings of heaviness or lack of motivation
- A sense of disconnection from the world

What You May Think

- "I don't know who I am without them."
- "Life doesn't feel the same anymore."
- "Everything feels harder now."
- "I feel like I'm moving through mud."

These experiences are not signs that something is broken. They are indicators that you are touching the deepest layers of your grief, where healing begins.

The Physical Weight of Sadness

Grief is not only emotional — it is physical.

People experiencing grief-related depression often report:

- Low energy or fatigue
- Difficulty sleeping or sleeping too much
- Body aches or tension
- Chest heaviness
- Changes in appetite
- Difficulty concentrating
- Slowed movements or restlessness

This is because grief activates the brain's stress response. The body is working hard to process trauma, sadness, and emotional shock.

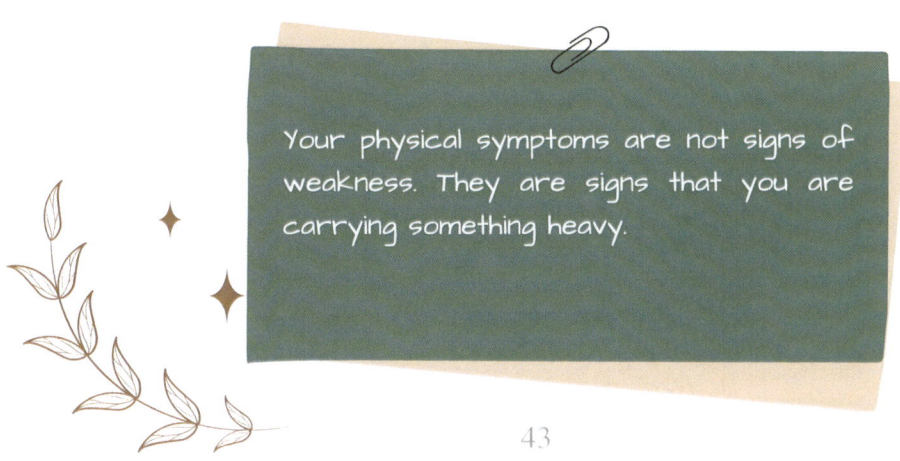

Your physical symptoms are not signs of weakness. They are signs that you are carrying something heavy.

The Purpose of Depression in Healing

Though depression feels like a low point, it is actually a place of transformation.

It Allows Full Emotional Recognition
You no longer deny what happened. You are acknowledging the true impact of the loss.

It Creates Emotional Space to Reflect
Depression slows the mind and softens the noise of daily life, allowing you to examine your inner world.

It Honors the Love Behind the Pain
Sadness exists because the connection mattered.

It Initiates the Search for Meaning
You may begin asking deeper questions about life, purpose, relationships, and what comes next.

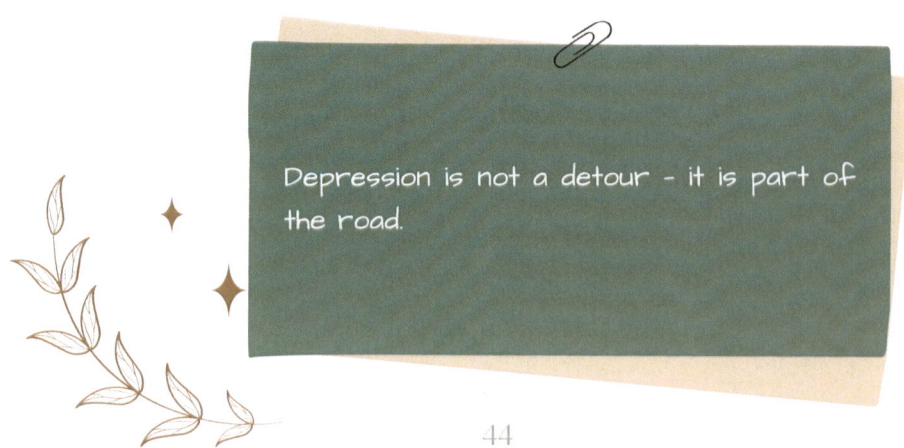

Depression is not a detour - it is part of the road.

Healthy Depression vs. Clinical Depression

Understanding the differences helps guide what kind of support may be needed.

Healthy Grief Depression

- Comes in waves
- Eventually softens with support
- Allows moments of relief or clarity
- Does not fully impair functioning
- Gradually transitions toward acceptance

Clinical Depression

Seek help if you experience:
- Feeling hopeless most days
- Suicidal thoughts or self-harm
- Complete withdrawal from life or responsibilities
- Total loss of interest in everything
- Persistent numbness or despair
- Inability to care for basic needs

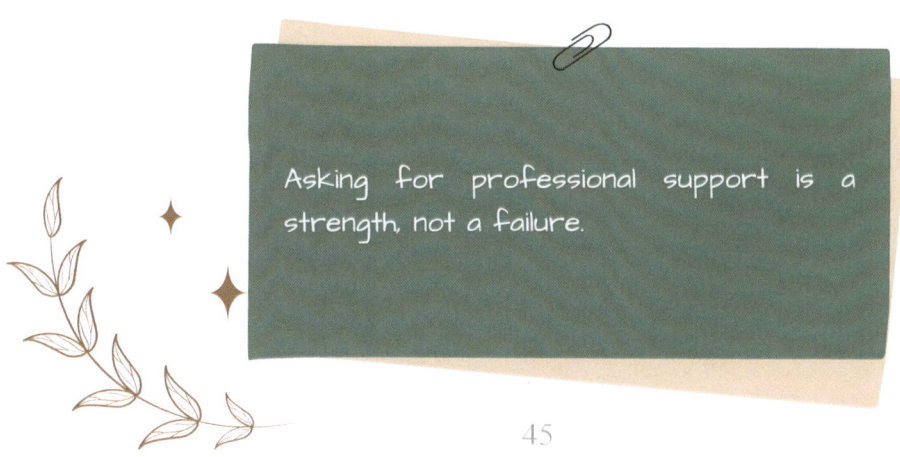

Asking for professional support is a strength, not a failure.

Secondary Losses: The Hidden Layers

Depression often intensifies because you are grieving not only the primary loss but also secondary losses attached to it.

Examples of Secondary Losses

- Loss of identity ("Who am I now?")
- Loss of routines or roles
- Loss of future plans or expectations
- Loss of financial security
- Loss of companionship or intimacy
- Loss of community or support systems
- Loss of stability and predictability

These losses compound emotional pain and deepen the heaviness you feel. Acknowledging them helps you understand why this stage feels so overwhelming.

Depression Across Ages

Grief affects different age groups in distinct ways:

Children
- May seem "fine" but show behavioral changes
- Have difficulty expressing or identifying emotions
- Often regress temporarily (sleep, habits, fears)

Teens
- May withdraw, become irritable, or appear disinterested
- Struggle with identity and role changes
- Feel isolated or misunderstood

Adults
- Carry multiple responsibilities while grieving
- Experience conflict between functioning and emotional exhaustion
- Often suppress feelings to support others

Older Adults
- Feel compounded losses (friends, health, independence)
- May isolate due to lack of social support
- Experience deeper reflection on life, legacy, and purpose

Each group needs understanding, patience, and unique forms of support.

The Spiritual Experience of Depression

Grief may stir spiritual questions:
- *"Why did this happen?"*
- *"Where was God in this moment?"*
- *"Why does my heart feel so heavy?"*

Some people feel disconnected from their faith. Others feel drawn closer to it. Both experiences are normal.

Spiritual Support Can Include:

- Prayer
- Scripture or inspirational readings
- Speaking with clergy
- Contemplative silence
- Soul journaling
- Worship or meditation
- Nature walks or quiet reflection

There is no "right way." Your spiritual journey is yours alone.

Coping Strategies: Gentle Ways Forward

Below are supportive techniques that help you move through this emotional stage with compassion and care.

- Create a simple, flexible routine
- Allow tears and emotional expression
- Reach out for support
- Practice mindful rest
- Engage in low-energy activities
- Seek pastoral or professional help
- Use journaling or guided reflection

Use this space to jot down your thoughts, feelings, or anything you'd like to practice from the techniques above.

Create a Simple Daily Routine

Depression often disrupts normal rhythms, making even basic tasks feel overwhelming. A gentle, flexible routine can provide structure without adding pressure.

- Start with three basic anchors each day: wake time, meals, and a moment outdoors.
- Keep habits small and manageable—shower, drink water, or dress comfortably.
- Use guiding habits instead of strict scheduling (e.g., "I will breathe fresh air today").
- Routines bring calm to emotional chaos, helping the body feel safer and more grounded.

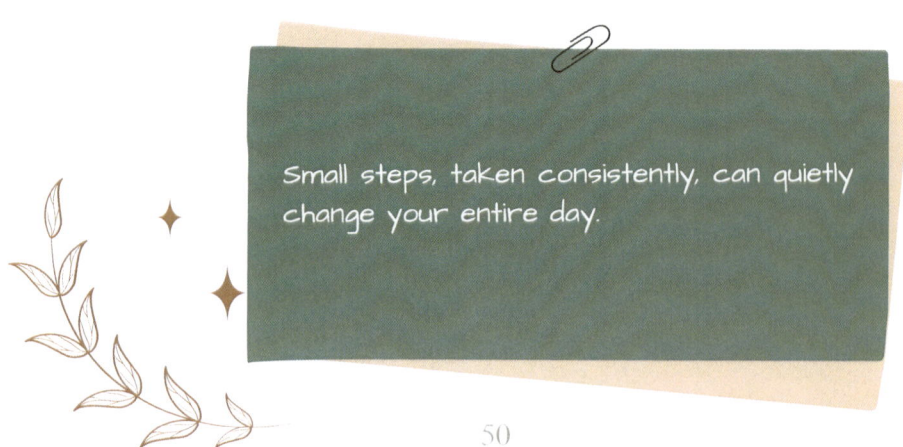

Small steps, taken consistently, can quietly change your entire day.

Allow Yourself to Cry & Reach Out for Support

Allow Yourself to Cry

Tears are a natural release for emotional pain.
- Crying releases stress hormones and regulates emotion.
- You may cry suddenly or quietly — all forms are valid.
- Tears do not mean you are breaking down; they mean you are healing.

Reach Out for Support

You don't have to grieve alone.
- Reach out to a trusted person, even if you only say, "I'm having a hard day."
- Presence matters more than perfect words.
- Support from family, clergy, friends, or counselors reduces emotional weight.
- Let others help with meals, tasks, or company — accepting help is strength.

Practice Mindful Rest & Low-Energy Engagement

Practice Mindful Rest

Depression brings emotional and physical exhaustion.
- Give yourself permission to slow down.
- Sit quietly, pray, meditate, or breathe deeply.
- Use grounding techniques: feeling your feet on the floor, placing a hand over your heart, or counting your breaths.
- Remind yourself gently: "I only need to take the next small step today."

Engage in Low-Energy Activities

Reconnect with life gently.
- Sit outside in fresh air
- Doodle, color, or write one simple sentence
- Listen to calming music
- Drink something warm
- Light a candle or water a plant

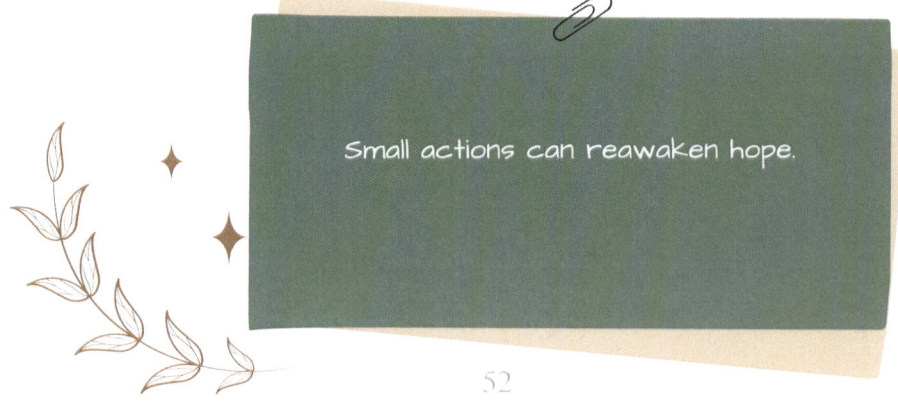

Small actions can reawaken hope.

Seek Support & Healing Exercise

Seek Professional or Pastoral Support

If your depression feels heavy or unmanageable:
- Speak with a grief counselor
- Join a grief support group
- Meet with a pastor or spiritual leader
- Ask your doctor for additional support

People I can call and lean on when I need help:

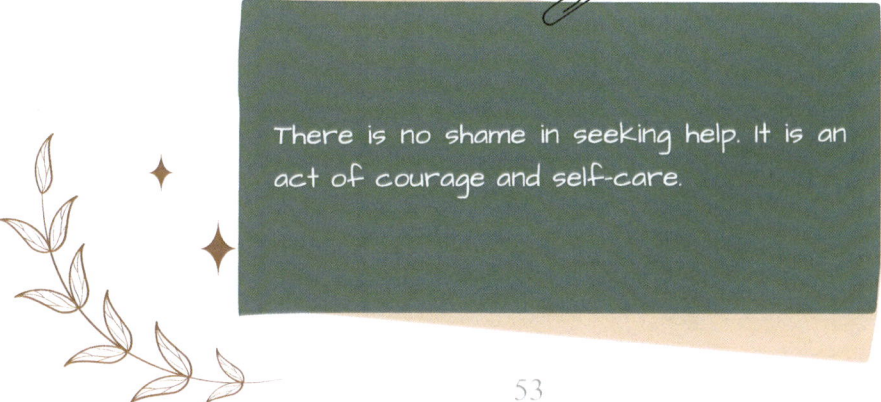

There is no shame in seeking help. It is an act of courage and self-care.

Healing Exercise

Write two lists:

1. "What I Miss Most."
2. "What I Am Learning About Myself Through This Pain."

These lists acknowledge both your loss and your emerging strength.

Supporting Someone in This Stage

If you are caring for someone who is grieving:

- Listen without trying to fix their pain
- Avoid phrases like "Be strong" or "You'll get over it"
- Offer consistent presence
- Help with practical tasks
- Validate their emotions
- Encourage professional support when appropriate
- Understand that depression is not a lack of faith or effort — it is grief

Your compassion can be a lifeline.

Transitioning Toward Acceptance

Depression is not the destination. Slowly, over time, signs of healing will emerge:

- A moment of laughter
- A day with less heaviness
- The ability to remember without overwhelming pain
- Hope returning in small ways
- Feeling ready to engage with life again

You are not forgetting your loved one or loss. You are learning to carry it differently — with strength, with meaning, and with love.

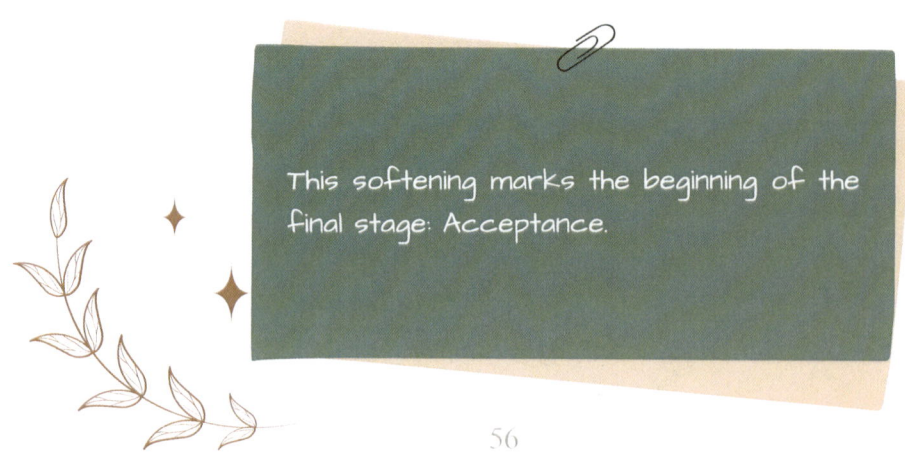

This softening marks the beginning of the final stage: Acceptance.

CHAPTER 5: STAGE FIVE

Acceptance

"Cast all your anxiety on him because he cares for you."

—1 Peter 5:7

Understanding Acceptance: A New Beginning, Not an Ending

Acceptance is often misunderstood. Many believe it means "being okay" with the loss or "moving on" as if the person or situation no longer matters. But acceptance is not the end of grief — it is the beginning of learning how to live with it.

Acceptance does not mean forgetting. Acceptance does not mean the pain disappears. Acceptance does not mean the loss becomes small.

Acceptance is the stage where you begin to understand that:

- Life has changed
- You cannot go back
- And you are learning how to live with both love and loss together

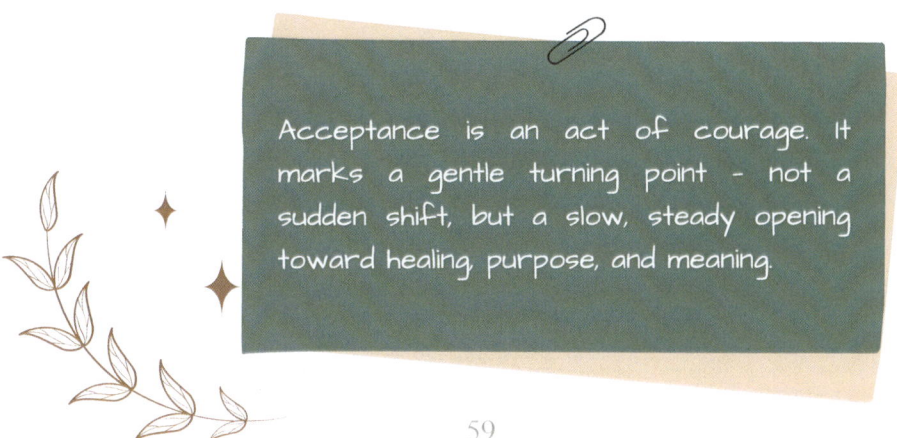

Acceptance is an act of courage. It marks a gentle turning point - not a sudden shift, but a slow, steady opening toward healing, purpose, and meaning.

What Acceptance Really Feels Like

Acceptance is quiet. It arrives in subtle ways, often unnoticed until you look back and realize how far you've come.

It may feel like:

- Taking a deep breath without breaking down
- Having a day where sadness feels softer
- Feeling ready to re-engage with life
- Making new plans for the future
- Laughing without guilt
- Remembering your loved one with warmth instead of only pain

Acceptance does not erase grief — it simply changes your relationship with it.

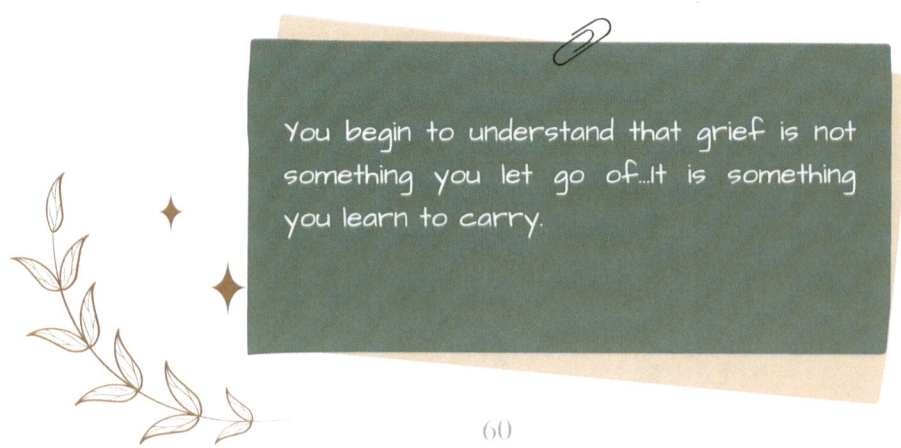

You begin to understand that grief is not something you let go of...It is something you learn to carry.

The Emotional Landscape of Acceptance

Acceptance brings a mix of emotions, not only peace.

Common Emotional Experiences

- Gratitude for the love you shared
- Sadness that still rises at times
- Relief from emotional exhaustion
- Curiosity about the future
- Renewed confidence
- Hope returning slowly
- A sense of stability or grounding
- A desire for new routines or connections

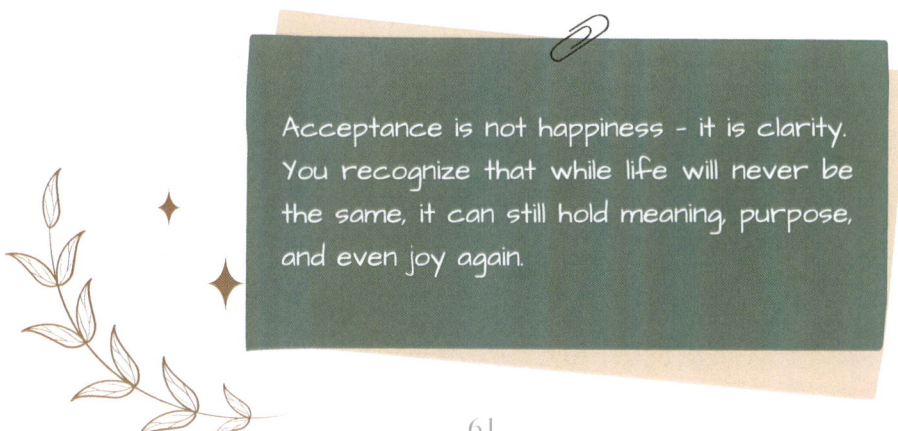

Acceptance is not happiness – it is clarity. You recognize that while life will never be the same, it can still hold meaning, purpose, and even joy again.

Letting Go of What Cannot Be Changed

This stage often brings a gentle understanding:

"I can't change what happened...but I can choose how I live from here."

Letting go is not abandoning your memories. Letting go is releasing the belief that life will return to what it once was.

Acceptance involves:

- Letting go of guilt
- Letting go of unrealistic expectations
- Letting go of past bargaining or "what if" thoughts
- Letting go of the belief that grief must disappear to live fully

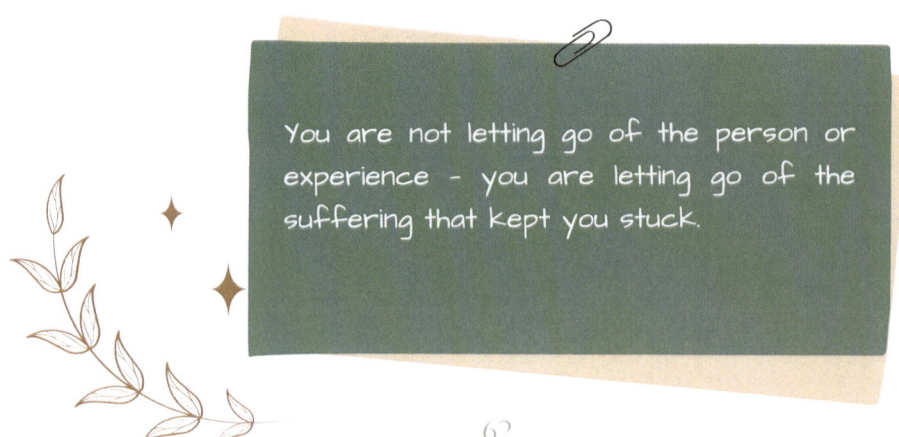

You are not letting go of the person or experience - you are letting go of the suffering that kept you stuck.

Acceptance Across the Grieving Mind

Acceptance may bring new clarity and reflection:

New Understanding
You see the loss with honesty, without trying to change it.

New Balance
You can feel sadness without losing yourself in it.

New Meaning
You recognize how the experience has shaped you — your values, compassion, and strength.

New Identity
You begin to understand who you are now, after the loss.

The mind becomes more settled. Thoughts slow down. You begin to choose your days rather than simply endure them.

Signs You Are Entering Acceptance

Acceptance is not a moment — it's a gradual transition.

You may notice:

- You think about the loss without breaking down
- You speak about your loved one freely
- You feel ready to return to work, school, or activities
- You make decisions with more confidence
- You regain a sense of routine
- You smile at memories instead of avoiding them
- You stop fighting the reality of what happened

Acceptance often feels like you're finally breathing again.

Building a Life After Loss

Acceptance invites you to rebuild. Not to replace what was lost, but to create life in a way that honors your journey.

This may include:

- Creating new routines
- Developing new goals or dreams
- Reconnecting with people
- Exploring new hobbies
- Traveling or reshaping your environment
- Growing spiritually
- Finding your voice and strength again

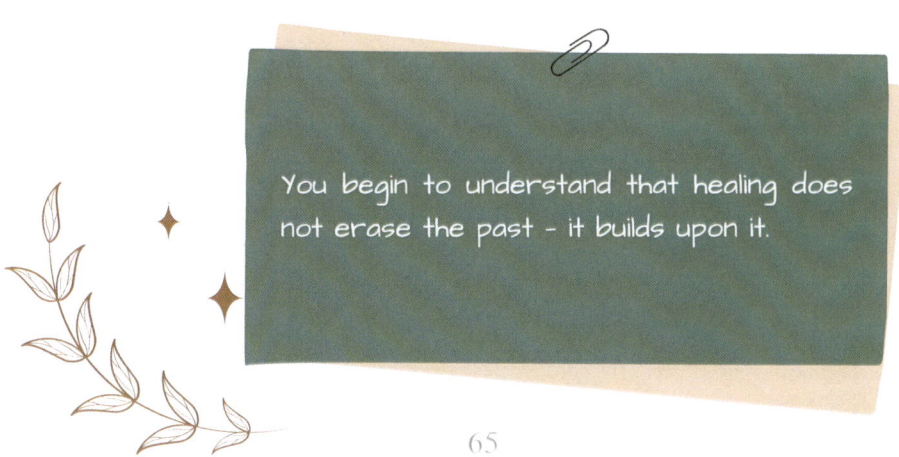

You begin to understand that healing does not erase the past - it builds upon it.

Continuing Bonds: Staying Connected in Healthy Ways

A key part of acceptance is realizing that you do not need to sever emotional ties with who or what you lost.

Healthy "continuing bonds" might look like:

- Keeping meaningful items
- Talking to your loved one in prayer or reflection
- Visiting special places
- Listening to their favorite music
- Creating traditions in their honor
- Telling their story
- Helping others in their memory

Acceptance invites connection - not disconnection.

Coping Strategies for Acceptance

Acceptance requires intentional nurturing. Below are practices that encourage growth and forward movement:

Create Meaningful Rituals
Light a candle, pray, journal, or visit a meaningful place regularly.

Practice Gratitude
Write down daily things — even small ones — that bring comfort or hope.

Redefine Your Purpose
Ask yourself: "What matters to me now?" Loss often reshapes priorities in powerful ways.

Create Balance
Allow moments of rest, connection, and creativity to coexist with grief.

Let Yourself Enjoy Life Again
Smiling, laughing, or experiencing joy is not betrayal — it is healing.

Spiritual Acceptance: Finding Peace in Faith

Acceptance often deepens spiritual reflection.

Common spiritual shifts:

- Feeling closer to God
- Seeking peace rather than answers
- Gaining clarity about purpose
- Understanding suffering in a new way
- Embracing gratitude and compassion
- Feeling guided toward healing

> Scripture, prayer, meditation, or quiet reflection may become comforting.
>
> Acceptance can bring a sense of spiritual grounding, reminding you that you are not walking alone.

Acceptance in Children, Teens & Adults

Children
- Show acceptance through routines and play
- May talk about the loss more openly
- Rebuild security gradually

Teens
- Reclaim identity and goals
- Seek meaning and independence
- May communicate acceptance indirectly

Adults
- Create new rhythms
- Rebuild purpose and direction
- Make long-term adjustments

Older Adults
- Draw on wisdom from past losses
- Often seek legacy, meaning, and peace
- Experience acceptance through storytelling and reflection

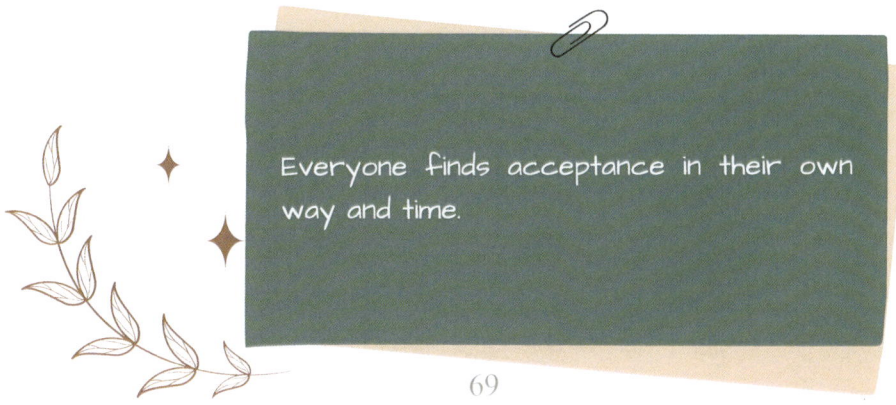

Everyone finds acceptance in their own way and time.

Helping Others Reach Acceptance

Acceptance cannot be rushed, but you can support others gently.

Ways to support someone entering this stage:

- Celebrate small signs of healing
- Encourage new routines or goals
- Be patient with emotional ups and downs
- Offer presence and reassurance
- Help them honor the past while embracing the future
- Listen with compassion
- Avoid minimizing their grief

Support is a powerful gift.

Acceptance and the Future: Living Forward

Acceptance allows you to imagine a future again — not a future without loss, but a future shaped by growth, resilience, and love.

This stage brings:

- Hope returning in small ways
- Energy to reengage socially
- Desire to create new memories
- Freedom from emotional heaviness
- Openness to new relationships or experiences
- A newfound appreciation for life's fragility and beauty

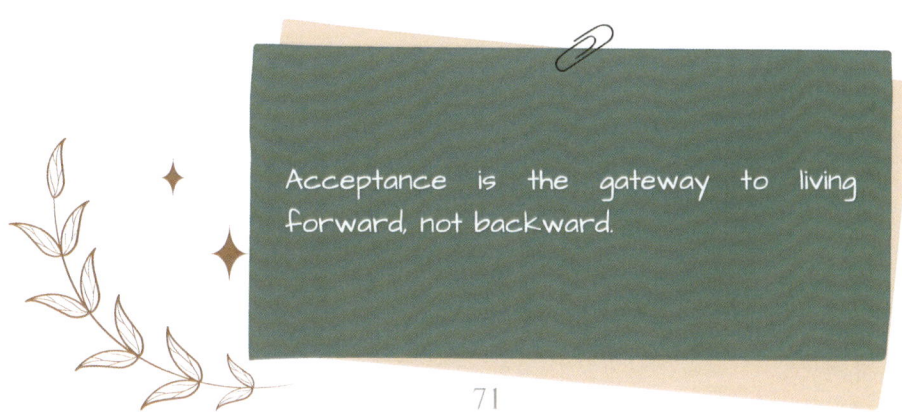

Acceptance is the gateway to living forward, not backward.

Healing Exercise

MY NEW CHAPTER

Who I Was Before the Loss
Reflect compassionately on the person you were.

Who I Am Now
Identify how grief has shaped your strength, insight, and character.

Who I Want to Become
Describe your hopes, goals, and vision moving forward.

One Step I Can Take This Week
Choose something small — a phone call, a walk, a prayer, or a moment of connection. Healing happens step by step.

A Gentle Closing: Grief Becomes Love in Motion

Acceptance is not a final stage — it is a lifelong unfolding.

You will continue to miss what you lost. You will continue to feel echoes of grief. But you will also continue to grow, love, and live with meaning.

And as you step into acceptance, you carry your love forward — not as pain, but as strength, wisdom, and purpose.

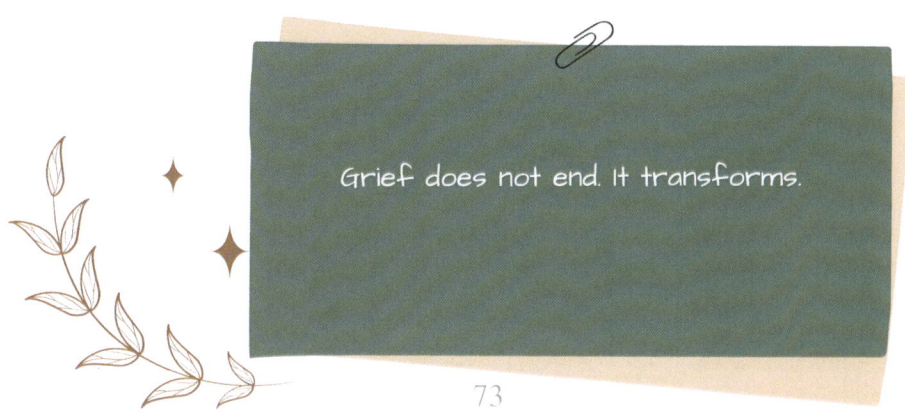

Grief does not end. It transforms.

Notes & Personal Reflections

What does acceptance mean to me today?

What small signs of healing have I noticed?

Who am I becoming through this journey?

What brings me comfort as I move forward?

Healing Tools, Activities & Daily Practices

"The Lord will guide you always; he will satisfy your needs in a sun-scorched land and will strengthen your frame. You will be like a well-watered garden, like a spring whose waters never fail."

— Isaiah 58:11

Memory Project

Use this page to honor a meaningful memory of your loved one:

- Recall a moment that still holds significance—something they did, taught you, or made you feel.
- Add a photo, drawing, or symbol that represents this memory.
- Write a few words about why this moment has stayed with you.

Keep this page somewhere you can return to whenever you want to feel close to them.

Reflection Prompts

Today I'm feeling...

I miss...

A comforting memory is...

Something that brings me peace...

Grounding Exercises

Box Breathing (4–4–4–4)

- Breathe in slowly through your nose for a count of 4.
- Hold your breath for a count of 4.
- Exhale slowly through your mouth for a count of 4.
- Pause and hold for a count of 4.
- Repeat for 3–5 rounds.

Grounding (5–4–3–2–1)

- Look around you and name 5 things you can see.
- Notice 4 things you can touch.
- Listen for 3 things you can hear.
- Notice 2 things you can smell.
- Name 1 thing you can taste (or imagine a favorite taste).

Gentle Movement / Walk

- Take a short walk, stretch your arms, or move slowly to release tension.
- Pay attention to your breath and your body as you move.
- Focus on how movement shifts your energy, even in small ways.

Journaling / Art / Music

- Write freely about your feelings, memories, or questions.
- Draw, paint, or create without worrying about the result.
- Listen to or play music that matches or soothes your mood.

Comfort Rituals

Use this page to create simple rituals that help you feel connected to your loved one. These can be daily, seasonal, or reserved for special dates—anything that offers comfort, remembrance, or a sense of closeness.

Ideas to inspire you:

- Light a candle in their honor
- Make a playlist of songs that remind you of them
- Visit a place they loved on a meaningful date
- Cook and share their favourite meal

Shape your rituals in a way that fits your life, culture, or faith—no matter how small, each one holds meaning.

CHAPTER 6

A New Path Forward

"May the God of hope fill you with all joy and peace as you trust in him, so that you may overflow with hope by the power of the Holy Spirit."

— Romans 15:13

A New Path Forward

As you come to the end of this book, your grief has not ended — but something has shifted. You have taken meaningful steps toward understanding your emotions, honoring your loss, and finding a deeper connection with yourself.

You have explored the stages of Denial, Anger, Bargaining, Depression, and Acceptance — not as rigid phases but as emotional landscapes that guide you toward healing. You have reflected on memories, acknowledged your pain, and recognized signs of resilience you may not have seen before.

Acceptance does not mean the absence of grief. It means learning to live with love in a new way.

As you move forward:

- There will be days when the ache feels heavy
- There will be moments when joy returns unexpectedly
- There will be memories that bring tears and others that bring warmth
- There will be growth, strength, and renewed purpose

A New Path Forward

Healing is not about forgetting. Healing is about integrating — carrying the love forward as you build a life shaped by grace, compassion, and courage.

Remember:

- You can take life one day at a time
- You can ask for help when you need it
- You can rest without guilt
- You can feel joy without betraying who or what you lost
- You can honor your grief while embracing your future

Your story is still unfolding.
Your strength is still rising.
Your heart is still healing.

As you walk into the days ahead, may you find peace in knowing:
You survived what you thought you never could. You are becoming someone stronger, wiser, and more compassionate. And you are worthy of the life you are stepping into.

This is not the end of grief. This is the beginning of living forward.

Because healing isn't rushed...It's supported.

RESOURCE GUIDE

Grief Forward™ Healing Manuals
(PRIMARY RESOURCES)

These manuals are written with compassion, clarity, and practical guidance to support individuals and families navigating grief.

Grief Forward™ Manual: Your Journey Toward Healing & Hope

A supportive guide that helps adults understand grief, explore emotions, and practice healthy coping strategies. Includes grounding exercises, reflective prompts, and gentle guidance for navigating the ups and downs of loss.

Grief Forward™ Manual: A Teen Guide for Healing, Growing & Moving Forward

An empowering teen-focused guide offering age-appropriate support for loss—including death, divorce, breakups, moves, and major life changes. Features relatable language, coping tools, journaling prompts, and emotional reflection activities.

These two manuals are ideal for individuals, families, support groups, churches, and schools seeking structured, compassionate grief support.

Resources

CRISIS & EMERGENCY SUPPORT

If you feel overwhelmed or unsafe:

- Call 988 immediately
- Reach out to a trusted friend or family member
- Contact your pastor
- Go to the nearest emergency room

You are never alone — help is always available.

EMOTIONAL & MENTAL HEALTH SUPPORT

Licensed Grief Counselors
- Bereavement specialists
- Trauma-informed therapists
- Christian counselors
- Sliding-scale therapy available through community centers

Grief Support Groups
- Funeral home–led groups
- Hospice grief programs
- Church grief ministries
- Online grief support meetings (Zoom/virtual)

24/7 National Hotlines
- 988 Suicide & Crisis Lifeline
- Crisis Text Line: Text HOME to 741741
- SAMHSA Mental Health Hotline: 1-800-662-HELP (4357)

Resources

FAITH-BASED & SPIRITUAL SUPPORT

Pastoral Care
- Church pastors and ministers
- Hospital chaplains
- Faith-based counseling
- Prayer and scripture support

Spiritual Healing Practices
- Devotional readings
- Prayer journaling
- Meditation or reflective silence
- Nature walks for grounding
- Gratitude-focused daily reflections

Faith Community Support
- Ministry groups (men, women, youth)
- Prayer circles
- Bible studies focused on hope and healing

BUILDING A SUPPORTIVE CIRCLE

Include people who help you feel emotionally safe:
- A close friend
- A trusted family member
- A pastor or spiritual mentor
- A grief counselor or therapist
- A grief companion (someone who understands your journey)

Healing is lighter when shared.

Resources

CHILDREN & TEEN GRIEF RESOURCES

Trusted Organizations
- Dougy Center (dougy.org)
- National Alliance for Children's Grief

Books for Youth
- Tear Soup — All ages
- When Someone Very Special Dies — Ages 6–12
- Healing Your Grieving Heart for Teens — Teen-focused

Signs a Child May Need Extra Support
- Behavior changes
- Sleep disturbances
- School difficulties
- Withdrawal or anger
- Persistent sadness

BOOKS & LITERATURE ON GRIEF

- On Grief & Grieving — Elisabeth Kübler-Ross & David Kessler
- Finding Meaning — David Kessler
- Healing After Loss — Martha Whitmore Hickman
- It's OK That You're Not OK — Megan Devine
- The Year of Magical Thinking — Joan Didion
- A Grief Observed — C.S. Lewis
- Through the Eyes of a Lion — Levi Lusko

Resources

SELF-CARE & WELLNESS RESOURCES

Helpful Apps
- Calm
- Headspace
- Abide (Christian-based)
- Insight Timer

Wellness Activities
- Gentle yoga
- Guided meditation
- Restorative stretching
- Breathing exercises
- Body relaxation routines

Nature & Movement
- Walk near water or trees
- Sit outside in sunlight
- Quiet reflection in nature

These practices reduce stress and support emotional healing.

References

Books & Foundational Works

- Kübler-Ross, Elisabeth, & Kessler, David. On Grief and Grieving: Finding the Meaning of Grief Through the Five Stages of Loss. Scribner, 2005.

- Kessler, David. Finding Meaning: The Sixth Stage of Grief. Scribner, 2019.

- Devine, Megan. It's OK That You're Not OK: Meeting Grief and Loss in a Culture That Doesn't Understand. Sounds True, 2017.

- Hickman, Martha Whitmore. Healing After Loss: Daily Meditations for Working Through Grief. HarperOne, 1994.

- Didion, Joan. The Year of Magical Thinking. Alfred A. Knopf, 2005.

- Lewis, C.S. A Grief Observed. Faber and Faber, 1961.

- Lusko, Levi. Through the Eyes of a Lion. Thomas Nelson, 2015.

Peer-Reviewed Research & Psychological Sources

- American Psychological Association. "Grief: Coping with the Loss of Your Loved One." APA Help Center, 2019.

- Bonanno, George A. "Loss, Trauma, and Human Resilience: Have We Underestimated the Human Capacity to Thrive After Extremely Aversive Events?" American Psychologist, vol. 59, no. 1, 2004, pp. 20–28.

- Stroebe, Margaret, & Schut, Henk. "The Dual Process Model of Coping with Bereavement: Rationale and Description." Death Studies, vol. 23, 1999, pp. 197–224.

- Worden, J. William. Grief Counseling and Grief Therapy: A Handbook for the Mental Health Practitioner. 5th ed., Springer Publishing, 2018.

Acknowledgments

I want to express my deepest gratitude to everyone who played a role in the creation of this book and in the development of the Grief Forward™ initiative.

To the families I've had the honor of serving through Cornerstone Funeral Services & Cremations —thank you for trusting me during the most difficult moments of your lives. Your courage, vulnerability, and love for those you've lost have shaped my heart and strengthened my calling. You have been my greatest teachers, and your stories live within every page of this work.

To my wife, LaQuisha, and our daughters —thank you for your unwavering support, patience, and encouragement. You are my strength, my motivation, and my reason for striving to serve others with compassion and excellence. Your love makes everything possible.

To my dedicated Cornerstone team —thank you for standing beside me in this sacred work. Your commitment to serving families with dignity and respect inspires me daily. This book reflects the heart of what we do together.

To our church family at The Star Church —your prayers, guidance, and spiritual covering have carried me through seasons of growth and purpose. Thank you for reminding me that service is ministry, and healing is a gift.

To the community leaders, educators, clergy, counselors, and professionals who have embraced the Grief Forward™ resources —thank you for believing in this vision and helping it reach those who need it most.

And finally, to every grieving heart who will read this book —thank you for allowing me to walk with you. Your pain is honored here. Your healing matters. Your journey is sacred.

May these pages bring comfort, clarity, and hope as you continue moving forward, one gentle step at a time.

About the Author

Bernard C. Buggs Jr. is the owner and managing funeral director, embalmer, and cremationist of Cornerstone Funeral Services & Cremations in Birmingham, Alabama. A retired Fire Lieutenant with the Birmingham Fire & Rescue Service Department and a proud Army veteran, Bernard has dedicated his life to serving families with compassion, dignity, and excellence during their most difficult moments.

He holds a Bachelor of Science in Fire Science and a Master of Business Administration with a concentration in Public Administration from Columbia Southern University, as well as an Associate in Applied Science in Funeral Service Education from Jefferson State Community College. Bernard is an active member of the National Funeral Directors Association, the Alabama Funeral Directors Association, and multiple professional development organizations committed to elevating funeral service standards. He is also a Charter Member of Kappa Alpha Psi Fraternity, Incorporated, Trussville-Pell City Alumni Chapter, where he continues to serve the community with distinction.

His dedication to quality, innovation, and compassionate care has earned Cornerstone multiple honors, including back-to-back NFDA Pursuit of Excellence Awards and CommunityVotes recognitions. Through these achievements, Bernard continues to raise the bar for funeral service in Alabama.

Bernard is also the creator of the Grief Forward™ Series — a growing collection of healing resources designed to support individuals, families, and teens as they navigate grief, loss, and emotional healing. His work is rooted in the belief that grief should never be rushed, minimized, or faced alone. With empathy, education, and lived experience, he provides accessible guidance that honors both the pain of loss and the hope of healing.

A devoted husband, father of three daughters, and active member of The Star Church, Bernard's life reflects a mission of service, faith, and community. He continues to find purpose in uplifting others through heartfelt care, education, and encouragement.

"Because healing isn't rushed... it's supported."